Usborne

Bugs
Magic Painting
Book

Illustrated by
Andy Tudor

Designed by Nelupa Hussain

To stop water from seeping through to
the next page, unfold the flap at the
back of the book and place it under the
page you're about to work on.

Dip the brush into
water, then brush it
across the black patterns
and lines within each
shape to see the paint
magically appear.